LIBRA HOR(

Your essential guide to love, money, happiness and using moon magic!

Hi guys,

A warm welcome to all my regular readers and a special hello to all new readers. I aim to provide a comprehensive insight into 2023 with spiritual, psychological insight, and down to earth common sense advice.

Every year when I write these books I just cannot believe how fast the year has gone, and that it's once again time to write and publish the series for the next year.

As many of you know, I've been producing these books since 2014, and boy has the world changed since then and 2023 will be a year of unprecedented change in world terms, that's why I've decided to also do an Astrology book of World predictions which include predictions for countries and certain leaders, because I feel that we need to be forwarded and for armed.

It's important to remember that no matter what is happening in the outside world, we all have our lives to live and karma to resolve and we must enjoy our own unique journey. Remember, we are all meant to be here at this very time, to experience what we are experiencing and we should never underestimate our own power and ability to thrive and make a difference.

Yes, we are all at different points along our own personal journey, but what I want to do with these books is encourage you all to understand your own creativity, power and never to underestimate yourself, to feel lost all to lose a sense of purpose. We are all here for a reason and we all have a valuable contribution to make in different ways, and hopefully my annual books have inspired you to understand your purpose and connect with some inspiration.

Fortunately the Saturn Square Uranus that was happening between Saturn in Aquarius and Uranus in Taurus is now done and dusted, which is a good thing because that was creating an enormous amount of tension within all of us, because the energies of Saturn and Uranus are so different. However, what we have coming this year is Pluto moving into Aquarius, and every time Pluto has changed signs there have been dramatic events worldwide that have changed history: it could be the birth of new countries, technological changes, conflict, economic shifts, innovations and the advent of new philosophies or political systems. So we should all be ready to embrace change with an open mind and we should remember not to be overly concerned with things that we are not able to change, because what we all can change is our attitude and it's always better to be optimistic and proactive.

I've often seen in my career as an astrologer that astrology works best for people who make plans, who act on those plans, who motivate themselves and who don't wait around for things to happen. Good things happen when we take chances, when we get up and seize opportunities or even just envisage then, very little happens we stick to comfort zones, resist change and hang onto the past for dear life, irrespective of the planets.

I always believe that it's important to understand our roots, to know where we come from and how our experiences have shaped us and given us wisdom. Our cumulative heritage is always important, but we can't live in the past, things are changing and we have to keep moving along and adapting, and using our wits and innate dynamic energy to thrive.

Love Lisa

This is a really good year for relationships for Libra. Jupiter enters into Aries after its retrograde period right at the start of January, and this brings a surge in positive energy into relationships, so the New Year is an excellent time for you and your partner to turn over a new leaf. If the relationship hasn't been going so well this is an excellent year to start marriage counselling, or if the relationship is going well, but it's lost a little bit of the old excellent, it's time for setting new goals which will motivate and stimulate the relationship.

If you and your partner have been struggling in anyway, say financially, this is also a time when brand new opportunities, different ideas and new perspectives can help increase your awareness on how to improve your financial situation and to become more prosperous, and there is a sense of help being on the way and a certain tide changing and luck improving.

If you and your partner have been struggling together with other emotional issues, this is also a time of healing where a fresh start can be made. So it's very important for Libra and your partner to turn over a new leaf, to go into 2023 with a new positive attitude, with a spirit of forgiveness and ready to embrace this year as a brand new start.

In general, this is quite a golden year for Libra because with Jupiter being in your solar 7th house, which is incidentally naturally the house of Libra, it gives you an opportunity to do the things you love most i.e. work with people, collaborate on projects, meet new people and mediate or act as a diplomat.

Your advice, your wisdom and your experience tends to be in demand, so careers where you offer work as a consultant or expert are certainly favored. This also helps you in legal careers, or in any legal matters you may be involved in.

While affairs of the heart are definitely assisted by Jupiter, Jupiter also helps you to have more positive supportive relationships with people in general, and this can also assist you in meeting new people to form business partnerships that will be very beneficial to you.

Boom not bust

Jupiter in Taurus later in the year indicates some good financial news, you may be able to secure a loan, reorganize your debt or apply for benefits or tax rebates, this is also a time when you may have success with insurance claims.

Later in the year is also a good time for your passive income, be it royalties, dividends, donations or possibly increased subscriptions to your website or any blogs or social media activity that you have.

"If you want my body and you think I'm sexy"

Later in the year is an excellent time for your sex life, so in new and existing relationships the excitement level in the sex life goes up dramatically. You may feel slightly more experimental, and there's a renewed level of interest in the intimate sphere.

Libra is a romantic and you're into meaningful relationships, but often you can be a little bit more restrained in terms of the sexual arena, but this year you're more likely to let your hair down, and to be able to let go, open up and enjoy sex on a more passionate and tantric level.

Losing control but awakening your hidden passion

Libra typically exhibits an enormous amount of self-control, you have a huge amount of restraint which makes you an incredibly strong character. You also have an iron will, but sometimes your emotions are buried so deep that you don't get to experience them to the full extent or explore them. So this year it's really important for you to do a deep dive emotionally and begin to untangle and unlock a lot of the deeply buried emotions that you may never think about.

In 2023, the key to really kick starting a dynamic new phase to your life and your relationships, and enabling you to connect with a partner at a deeper level is simply because you are expressing your emotions with so much more clarity and confidence.

It's a year of refreshment and renewal

In 2023, the North node and Uranus continue to be in Taurus along with Jupiter later in the year, which conjuncts the North node, this is a symbol of renewal and replenishment in your life.

This is a very important year for you to eliminate what is toxic, but you need to do this in holistic way. So this can be an excellent year for diet, detoxing and going on a health kick much more based around natural and organic produce. It's definitely time to move away from highly manufactured toxic goods, and if you have any bad habits like smoking and drinking you're able to quit. It's definitely a year when you are more able to tackle psychological issues, to access your deep levels of determination and to move away from those addictions.

Sex is a stairway to heaven

A new sexual relationship could be the catalyst to a great awakening, so while relationships based around sex alone are usually not what Libra is looking for, this year sexual relationships, even if they don't last or even if they are 'friends with benefits' relationships, can have a role, and can help awaken something within you which alerts you to the potential for a better future via different attitudes at a fundamental level. So sex is like a gateway drug to higher spiritual understanding and enlightenment.

You're enigmatic

Libra can be a little bit secretive and sometimes withdrawn this year, this could be due to the fact that you're thinking a lot more about deeper issues and needs and these thoughts niggle or trouble you. Libra is one for sweeping things under the carpet, but eventually as we know, anything that gets stashed away in the attic, the basement or of course under the carpet, has to be dealt with eventually, and it's usually not such a fun process. So if you need a bit of privacy and space, that's what you are dealing with, the gross stuff under the carpet.

On a more mundane level, doing a great big clear out, getting more organized, getting rid of old junk or items from your past etc. can be an important part of a cleansing process. Clear-outs are not the entire part of an internal cleansing process, but often if there are tangible or material items around your home that keep reminding or tying you to something in the past, it can be quite helpful to burn them or get rid of them.

The sun will come out tomorrow, so you gotta hang on til tomorrow

Libra may have this nagging feeling that you're come to the end of a major phase in your life, and this is quite apropos, as Pluto has been squaring the sun of all Librans from Capricorn over the past 14 years, but as it moves into Aquarius in 2023, it means a whole era for Libra has ended and so there's no doubt that this is going to be the dawn of something valuable and important happening.

Taking it like an adult

2023 is also a time for you to set aside immature things and attachments, put the past behind you and embrace new opportunities and possibilities, simply because that is the way for transformation to come into your life.

Libra must begin to embrace the entire spectrum of emotions within you, rather than focusing on the light and denying the shadow. You cannot hide behind diplomacy and politeness as some eggs have to be broken to make the 2023 omelet. Libra is conflict avoiding by nature, but in 2023 you must be more confrontational and even ruthless in order to justify a brand new start and to make it cleanly. Ruthlessness means decisiveness and the eagerness to take action and cut ties where necessary with people or places.

Using your innate creativity to create fertile ground for new love

You need to begin to understand how holding on to things, whether it's material things, grudges, romantic attachments or certain unhelpful friends, actually creates more pain in your life, both emotionally and physically.

Part and parcel of your great new beginning is using your creative imagination to visualize exactly where you want to be, so this year is a whole new opportunity to reimagine your life and all the possibilities attached to that.

Money Matters

As Uranus is involved with the North Node in your solar eighth house, there can be sudden and unexpected change to do with finances. This is usually an indirect force, so your partner may change jobs leading to a change in their finances which may impact on you, or changes in the wider social and economic sphere particularly with interest rates, costs and inflation may cause changes to the way you run your business, invest or conducts your debt.

Often dealing with these sudden and unexpected financial situations can lead to you having to restructure your thinking and your priorities, which leads to quite an emotional upheaval and change as well. So often things that started out as a money concern end up leading to emotional changes which lead to emotional cleansing and sudden realizations about what your true needs really are.

The winds of change should be welcomed

Libra really likes to feel in control, you are a person who's very organized, who likes to be prepared and who doesn't particularly like change be it with people, in relationships, in business or your life, although sometimes this year you will feel at sea as if you are caught up in a tsunami of change and you cannot escape its effects. However, you need to go with it, you need to learn the lesson of flexibility and adaptability, and you need to learn that you can't control or manage everything - that is a big lesson for you in 2023.

Change and upheaval should not be associated in your mind with failure, as it is opportunity and you need to disconnect those words in your head, so that you are more positive about sudden unexpected changes and upheavals.

Disappearing act

In some cases, something unexpected could bring an end to problems you have had or some problems suddenly disappear and new problems appear. However, problems are part of life and they are always linked with an opportunity, so again it's a case of being positive about these and proactive.

Talking of disappearing, this is the perfect time for habit breaking and establishing new positive habits. Habits can be good or bad, so it's good to replace an old bad habit with a new good habit.

The Changing nature of work

Significant organizational change or structural change in the economy could impact the way you work or the organization you work for. So you need to work with colleagues and use your mediation and diplomatic skills to help everyone adapt to change. Thus whatever your previous role in your work was, you may find that you are busier with teamwork and team leadership this year, rather than the goals you normally fulfill. Libra can also play an important role in motivating and encouraging people to deal with change and upheaval or restructuring.

Change management, grief counselling and other forms of career that involve reorganization or helping people cope with change. These are all avenues you can explore.

Looking out for love

If you are looking for love, this is a year when fate is about to step in and give you a little nudge in the right direction. Now Libra likes to be involved in long, close and committed relationships, you don't usually let fate take care of it, you tend to be proactive about your love life, but this year something may happen that is unexpected that leads to you having a passionate and almost obsessive relationship with a new person.

Meeting at the crossroads

It may be possible that you meet someone who is at a crossroads in their life, and it just happens that you and the other person meet at a time when you are both closing one chapter and ready to start another chapter. This means that you are both very open to exploring new ground and more available to each other than you might have been previously, because you are both in uncharted waters which can also make you both more open, allowing the relationship to become deep, intimate and passionate much more quickly.

Assistance is on the way

Jupiter in Aries brings a lot of healing to struggling relationships, but as Jupiter goes into Taurus, new perspectives and a deeper level of willingness to let go of the negatives in the past and to begin thinking more about the future and how you can come together through the shared values and priorities you have dawn.

Running hot

Mars will be in Gemini, which represents your solar ninth house, for the first 2 months of the year and into March.
This is very positive for Libra because it allows you an opportunity to promote yourself, extend your reputation and gain much needed publicity for either yourself, your ideas or your products.

During this space you will do more creative intellectual work than usual, which is particularly rewarding for a Libra, being an air sign, as you will experience new insights in terms of society and politics, and you will be able to assimilate that and express these views to others.

The Mars in Gemini is excellent for any Libra who have decided to enter a new field, and who have to do some studying or engage in a steep learning curve to master new skills, or to adapt for a new job. So this is certainly an energetic time in terms of academic and intellectual learning, which will help you to quickly progress in a new field and find your feet.

So excited and you just can't hide it

Mars in your 9th solar horse represents a certain amount of adventure, therefore you are a lot more gung ho, ambitious and excitable. You're also more willing to take risks and that can help you in business as you seize opportunities that you wouldn't normally see.

Being quite impulsive you like to jump in at the deep end and you're certainly got enough gusto and oomph to swim to the surface and tread water while you begin to understand what you're got yourself into.

You're often a bit of an adrenaline and excitement junkie at the beginning of the year, this can help you because you smash out of comfort zones and try new things in love and life, but at the same time you can be a little bit reckless and this can lead to some quite dramatic mistakes, but you're always ready to jump back on the horse and ride again.

Driving your point home

You can be very persuasive and your influence over other people increases, which means that if you need to put forward certain opinions or to try and educate or inform people, you can grab their attention, hold it and ram the message home, although you must try not to be too dogmatic, because sometimes you can come over as pushy or a little bit domineering in your attitudes.

The problem with the beginning of the year is you don't always stop to self-censor, sometimes you can be a little bit like a runaway train and you're not got the self-awareness to know when you're going too far, exaggerating or biting off more than you can chew.

However the luck tends to flow with you, and you are able to create a little bit of excitement for yourself, whilst always being able to get out of a danger.

Rising up to the challenge of your rival

The start of the year is a great period for any sporting and self-improvement goals, you get a lot of satisfaction out of sporting events, especially those that happen in the great outdoors. You enjoy testing your skills against others, be it your physical or intellectual skills, so you love the cut and thrust of competition.

Libra should be looking for all opportunities to take it on and see what you can do in a competitive arena.

Understanding your obsessions

It's very important for you to examine any obsessive behavior or any crutches that you have. You need to think more clearly about why you rely so heavily on certain things and what value they fulfil, if any in the current context. It's time for you to let go of those crutches as they may be holding you back more than helping you at this stage, and that's why you need to think about their true purpose and genesis.

Libra actually finds it a lot harder to let go than one would imagine for a cardinal sign. Librans are incredibly capable, they are often leaders, entrepreneurs and freethinkers, but at a deep level, they find it extremely hard to let go of certain things. There can be attachments to the past, hurts, angers and resentment, and you need to work very hard this year on letting go of all those things because they are also toxic.

Freeing up suppressed energy

This can be an excellent year for any kind of psychological therapy or counselling, simply because you're more able to access your hidden emotions and you have the impetus to resolve certain suppressed feelings or memories that maybe swimming around with no real direction, as a lot of your energy is being soaked up by these negative memories. So you need to kind of let them loose and set them free, thus beginning a cleansing process that will entail taking parts of yourself and letting them go - these could be parts of your past or those crutches - and letting them go and thus being willing to refresh your life through refreshing your thinking.

Twist in the tail

New relationships can have an unexpected effect on you, you can become a lot more emotional and like I said, many buried emotions come to the surface. However, because of this, you have to be very careful of not being emotionally manipulated by a partner who can sense that you are suddenly experiencing a surge of emotion and want to play on it.

Relationships can become rather overwhelming, simply because of the intensity, the level of passion and possibly because there are more vested interests and conflict than usual.

A new partner you connect with may represent something different to the people you would have connected with or fallen for before, and that's probably part of the reason why they bring out different aspects of your personality. However this can be very exciting for you, and also means that the sex life is that much more interesting because you're experimental and little bit more riske.

Crashing through your defenses

Although boundaries are important in a new relationship, a new partnership which actually challenges and breaks down your boundaries can be strangely cathartic for you. In some cases, you may have a brief yet incredibly passionate or volatile fling with someone, but that person may not to be permanent partner potential, but could rather be a catalyst for change. So it is possible that you have a wild yet brief encounter with someone who actually changes your perspectives and sets you free from the past.

In other cases a brand new relationship, like I say, which is very different comes along and you're swept adrift in a whirlwind, and then almost forget yourself, forget your old boundaries and develops a whole new way of relating and loving on an intimate level, which is a beautiful thing.

Finances

During the year Jupiter is square Pluto, it's an excellent signal for your finances, you should see organic growth and improvement in your business situation, and you make experience more demand for your products and services, or you may attract bigger clients.

This is definitely a time when the Goodwill in your business increases, you will experience enhanced reputation and may get good reviews or positive word of mouth that helps you to grow.

This year is particularly good for those of you in careers that involve teaching, publishing, travelling or activities related to the tourism industry.

This can also be a good year to invest in your business or in your skills. So if you work for someone, you may want to invest in training courses or higher learning. If you have your own business it might be wise to invest in assets, particularly if these are in energy saving.

It's obvious that wise use of resources is very important during this time, this is particularly salient for Libra, as your chances to succeed in business and prosper financially is strongly connected to your use of resources and thus it's more vital for you than other signs, to be energy efficient, and to make use of things you already have. It's also important to repair or restore things and manage carefully your use of resources as this is time well spent.

2023 is also a year to reward yourself, it's very important to set up goals and targets and to reward yourself when you have reached them. So it's quite sensible to have times of indulgence. Periods of austerity and saving should be alternated with times when you reward yourself, relax have a few luxuries and do things are truly make you feel pampered.

All work and no play makes Jack a dull boy, so make plenty of time for pleasure this year.

The windmills of your mind

It's quite ok to have a period of self-questioning but don't believe you're in the wrong. Some things may not have worked out, but that doesn't always mean you were right or wrong, sometimes it just means that you were complacent and missed a trick about something or perhaps something changed.

So cut yourself some slack, you should not be over critical, you should just understand that change is a natural part of life, and we can't have all the answers to all the questions all the time. In fact sometimes the questions change and we haven't realized it because we weren't paying attention, but as soon as you do pay attention you should find the solution. However, don't settle for superficial explanations, try and get as close to the inner workings of any element of a problem area as you can.

Short journeys that you don't expect to take, and sudden encounters with strangers can have a profound effect on you, so even something as mundane as a train ride or a commute to work could suddenly take an unexpected turn that could result in something from left field, which you couldn't have envisioned, but that will change your life in some way.

9-5

It's important to be observant, especially when it comes to your everyday life, because it is the details that can sometimes trip you up and cause problems. Don't take issues connected to neighbors, your relatives (like cousins and aunts and uncles) or any other routine administrative issues for granted, as all of these can impact you in different ways that are significant.

It's very important this year to be extremely diligent about administration, record-keeping and doing your due diligence.

This year details count and count a lot, and so you need to be abreast of the finer details, able to substantiate your arguments and your record keeping should mean you always have the necessary documentation to provide proof or evidence of your identity, your course of action and your reasoning.

This is a year when many situations that have been chugging along in the background, or you've been putting up with for years and have become a predictable part of your life, suddenly reach a crisis point, are no longer predictable or no longer work for you. This can create a significant crisis in day-to-day activities or the day-to-day running of your business.

So do watch out for things that you've always assumed will be there, or will work fine, suddenly not working and it being breaking down, this is particularly true for technology.

It's wise this year to always to have a backup plan and not to take anything for granted: people or machinery. Always be ready for something to fail or to surprise you in some way.

While there can be some surprises that are unpleasant and caused a lot of disruption, often surprises which come to light will provide solutions, so it's very important to be aware of new technology, new software programs and things which can actually assist you in positive ways, or even replace those accustomed ways of doing things you always relied on before.

Angels and Demons

This year Mercury is retrograde in Capricorn, Taurus and Virgo, and again in Capricorn at the end of the year, this will affect your solar 4th, 8th and 12th houses, these houses are all deeply personal houses.

The retrogrades this year all call for you to reflect and gain deeper self-understanding. In May and September particularly, it is important for you to have time alone. Yes I know this is a great year to be social, do things with other people and to expand via interactions with other people, but during May, September and December it is very important for you to have time to think, that means there's a space for you to look inward and two recap.

This year it's very important to keep a personal and private journal, you should be recording thoughts, feelings and how these are linked to events as you go through the year. It's very important for your self-awareness, personal growth and in a cathartic way also, to write things down.

It's also very important when rebalancing relationships and understanding better your interactions with others that you keep note of observations, feelings and events that have happened, and then you can frequently recap on these. This helps you get a grasp of the psychologically in terms of emotional awareness of the type of personality traits of the new people you are meeting, and the kind of behavior exhibited by your partner too

I mentioned that this is an excellent year for improving relationships, part of this is improving your own understanding and growing via your relationship, and you can do that better when you use certain time periods of the year for reflection. Keep reading your journal so that you can truly understand the positive changes that are happening, possible pitfalls and how you've overcome them, and any other observations which are key to gaining a better understanding in your life.

This is an excellent year for techniques like meditation because it's wise to be able to switch off your mind so that you can have a total mental reboot. It's also important to have some space alone so that you can get rid of the influences of other people, whether positive or negative, to reconnect with your core and understand whether you are on course.

So periodically, particularly in May and September, are ideal times for reflection and contemplation before you get back out there with a better understanding, in order to truly fulfil your purpose.

*Essence and Energies – "Play the game, you know you can't quit until
it's won
Soldier on, only you can do what must be done"*

The essence this month is purging and preparing for the unexpected.

*Librans are in the process of restructuring their lives; you are driven to get
organized and purge yourself of old relationships, habits, people and
places which no longer serve your needs. However you should not fall into
thinking that you suddenly have all the answers. Unexpected events will
force you to reassess and you should take a step back and ask yourself
what these events are trying to tell you.*

*In all walks of life do not take things at face value, look below the surface
and be more cynical about the motivations of others – surprises can come
from people who suddenly do an about turn and react unpredictably. Your
opponents and enemies are not to be underestimated: keep your eye on
their every move.*

*Affirmation: "I am unafraid to scratch the surface and see what I uncover,
I have no fear."*

Love and Romance

This month is quite complicated for love relationships as Libra may face a
freedom closeness dilemma. Single Libra should be working on their self-
worth and using creativity to satisfy any desires or needs of a romantic
nature. This is not the best time to start a brand new relationship as a new
relationship that begins right now could be quite heavy in terms of karma
and responsibility.

Libra who are in romances or dating at the moment should show more
patience and work harder at deepening the relationship. January by its very
nature tends to be a reflective month and a slightly sobering month, after
all the festivities in December, and in terms of your romantic relationships

this should also be a sober time where you seriously consider where the relationship is going and if it is viable.

You have been standing back from taking chances in new relationships, but when you connect with someone this year it will seem natural to let go and let your heart off the leash. This new relationship has the potential to be rather transformative for you; it may help boost you into a new phase in life or help you to take chances in other walks of life. Ideally it will nurture more security for you and this will be a springboard for other areas of your life.

Career and Aspiration

Mercury retrograde in your solar 4th house indicates this is a time of preparation and consolidation. This is a very good time for research and restructuring in terms of your business, this may also be a good time to sort out relationships with your suppliers or maybe find new suppliers. You need to think more about your supply chain or the essential inputs to your work and sure these up.

If you are in employment rather than in your own business, this may be a time where you have to do a lot of extra reading in order to get yourself up-to-date and get totally abreast of new situations. This is a very good time for Libra who are taking time out to study, as you have great focus, concentration and should find quite enough time to get fully prepared.

This is not an excellent time for public speaking, taking business trips or the running headlong into some new venture, everything should be thoroughly researched and thought through.

If you have a business idea this is also a highly opportune time to begin it as you will forge contacts and clients easily and have the mental ability to focus your activities and direct a strategic plan. Remember there is nothing as urgent as an "idea that has come." There are also many opportunities for teaching, counselling or lecturing – thus if you are a Libran with a skill, maybe it is time to find a college or university or course at some place of further learning where you can pass on your skills and expertise.

Adventure and Motivation

With Mars going direct in Gemini in your solar 9th house, this is an excellent month for your sporting and competitive goals. So this is a fine month for you to start new sporting activities, get involved in sports clubs or attend more social activities linked to sporting ventures.

Despite the cool weather in the Northern hemisphere and the hot weather in the Southern hemisphere, this is a still a great time for you to get outdoors, experience fresh air and be physically active in a space that is not enclosed like a gym or home gym.

You're quite opinionated this month and you often get a great deal of pleasure out of expressing your views on social media, or through publishing of blogs and this can also be quite a channel for your frustrations.

Marriage and Family

This month sun is conjunct Pluto in Capricorn indicating that there may be very important developments in the family which totally change the trajectory of the year. In fact important discussions may take place within the family about potential home moves or renovations, or issues facing family members. So it's important for everyone to spend time coming together as a family to discuss these issues, which will affect you all, and so open new opportunities and decide where to cut back.

Jupiter entering Aries at the beginning of the month is a wonderful sign for marriage, it encourages healing, corporation and restoration of commitment.

Whether your marriage is in an excellent state or struggling along, the Jupiter transit can definitely help improve your spirits had optimism, and bring an impetus of conciliation to help the relationship turn over a new leaf and enter a fulfilling and satisfying new phase.

Libra need to pay close attention to changes within their mates. Perhaps out of force of habit you know what to expect from them or you think that you know them so well you no longer need to pay close attention to their moods, however things are changing for them: their values, needs and perspectives are not static and if you are not aware of and do not adjust to these changes things could be difficult. Open your mind and begin to learn about your loved one again – this can be very exciting, like a rediscovery. For relationships that have been in difficulty this year could be a turning point where you either separate or where things turn the corner.

Money and Finance

With Mercury retrograde in Capricorn, this is not a good time to arrange any pensions or change your pension arrangements.

This is however a great month for a positive attitude in terms of budgeting and forward planning, you should be fairly optimistic in setting yourself targets and benchmarks to aim for, and you can also employ positive thinking and affirmations to get you into the right mindset for the year ahead in terms of work.

The key is for you to think big, for you to believe in yourself and for you to use the talents and abilities you have that are underutilized in order to supercharge your year.

In terms of finances, the key motto here is, 'get it done', so if there's anything pending you should act on it now.

Living and Loving to the Full

This month the keywords in terms of relationships are commitment, trust and communication. With the ruler of Libra, Venus in Aquarius conjunct Saturn, there's a great opportunity to bring romance and affection back into relationships, however without trust there can be a lack of security, which means that you both are held back in terms of self-expression.

The more Libra can make your partner feel secure, and likewise, the more love and romance blossoms simply because you both feel in a safe place in the relationship. So this month to enhance love magic, Libra must help your partner to develop confidence and self-worth, so that means complements and showing genuine affection and renewed levels of commitment.

Planetary Cautions

Mercury is retrograde in Capricorn until the 19th of the month, so until that time activities like house-hunting or planning home reservations are not favored. This is also not a good time to have relatives to stay, or to have any major work done on your home other than repairs.

In general this is not a favorable time for activities regarding real estate, with respect to your own property or if your career is real estate.

This is also a time to be more cautious in terms of businesses involving the environment, tourism, culture and hospitality.

Communication is very important within the family circle, but there should be no pressure on any member of the family to reach a decision, you guys should keep all your options open.

Moon Magic

The new moon phase extends from the 21th of January to the 5th of February, this waxing phase is the perfect fortnight for new initiatives, setting plans, establishing goals, starting anything prospective and being proactive. This is the action phase, details below:

Mercury goes direct on 19th indicating that the communications sphere, short journeys, job interviews, public speaking, teaching and research are again successful. Matters connected to property, real estate contracts, home improvements and family decisions can move forward.

Sun Sextile Jupiter at the new moon favors networking, groups goals and any high teq or scientific aims you have. This is good for political and social organizing. This also favors your social life and making new friends.

Venus Conjunct Saturn indicates a good time for family events and celebrations. This is excellent for new business based from your home or expanding your home office. Renovations and house hunting is successful.

This is not a favorable time for borrowing money, tax planning or managing new clients' money.

New romance, dating and social activities are not successful in the waxing phase. Brand new activities you're never tried before or new physical training is not successful.

Mars goes direct in Gemini on the 13th bringing about momentum for your promotional activities, competitive goals, higher education, publishing and team leadership.

Essence and Energies - "One flash of light, one God one vision"

The essence this month is the creative escape from the turmoil and destruction within, This is a time to harness discordant emotion and revive ambition, especially in artistic ventures.

It's important to seek renewal and escape from your own issues by challenging yourself to be more competitive and to pursue your creative hobbies or aspects of your career with more passion.

It's important to clear out the old cobwebs and to be serious about welcoming in something new to your work or creative life.

Often revelations can come in a flash of truth or inspiration, but you have to lay the foundation by embracing new activities with passion.

Affirmation: "I understand that I am a creative and unique individual and when I focus on my passion not my problems, amazing things happen."

Love and Romance

This a time when single Libra may play the field and actually enjoy having sexual encounters with different partners. Sometimes you just needs to sow wild oats and get something out of your system, so maybe you could be a little bit rebellious, and could have some brief and exciting affairs just to clear your head until you move into a zone when you feel more likely to want to commit.

In ongoing relationships, Libra can feel a little bit ambivalent, part of you wants to commit, but you're quite indecisive in love. Right now you're scared of losing your freedom, and you may be concerned that the person you are with right now could become controlling and possessive. So you certainly need to think long and hard about your current relationship and how to avoid any issues that will result in the relationship becoming restrictive and too formulaic.

Career and Aspiration

With Venus conjunct Neptune in your solar sixth house of work and service, this is an extremely successful time for Libra who work in compassionate and caring fields. This is a very good time for Libra who may be interested in following medical fields or who already work in any medical or pharmaceutical capacity.

If you are not in touch with your need for change and renewal, you may feel nervous and agitated, you could find it hard to settle or concentrate. It's important to acknowledge where your life is stale and in need of change and excitement.

Anything which no longer cuts mustard has to go, you must focus and show determination and it's amazing what you can achieve despite the odd being stacked against you.

Validation and confidence must always be sought within and while you will garner support from friends, cheerleaders and those who align with your cause, when push comes to shove you must be able to dig deep and tap into your faith in you and what you stand for.

Goals that do not matter on a deep level fall away but those which do matter cling to you and will not let you go even when you want to walk away. Sometimes during this month, the mission comes looking for you – you are the one it chooses and you are the woman for the job.

It's important for you to avoid office gossip and you should stay aloof from colleagues who are looking to agitate or get involved in any disputes. The key thing for you to remember this month, is your colleagues, your customers or your clients disputes or problems are not your own and you should not become immersed in their issues.

It's very important this month for you to know where to draw a line.

Adventure and Motivation

This month you can have a great deal of fun working in teams and collaborating with other people. Libra is a social person and it's particularly in evidence this month, so any activity that would help you to meet new friend or find causes in which you can unite with others is especially fulfilling.

You enjoy activities where you can do good deeds, help others out and give advice. Libra tends to be rather thoughtful and well informed and you love giving your opinion, and so any activity this month where you are able to impart your wisdom, play a mediator role or even a matchmaker role in love, brings you a lot of satisfaction.

However you do need to be a little bit careful that you are not interfering with other people, or throwing your pennies worth in where it is not wanted, because you can be a little bit OTT about importing advice

Marriage and Family

This is generally a positive time in marriages, there is indication that you and your partner can work well together, can improve your prosperity and can make progress on family matters, as long as you guys both work at the harmony and understanding level.

This is certainly a time when you are able to achieve more balance between your needs and the requirements of the relationship, but it's important for Libra to acknowledge the value your partner brings to the partnership too. Successful marriage right now relies on both partners feeling that they are equal, that their contributions are of equal worth and there is justice in the marriage. If one partner feels there is unfairness or double standards, then that certainly is a problem that needs to be addressed and worked on.

You are the solid, emotionally dependable one right now in love – somehow you have a better grasp of what is going on right now and are seeing reason. Your partner may turn to you increasingly this period due to your ability to truly understand their situation. It maybe that you know your partner better that he knows himself and are thus more clearly able to see where they are going wrong and how they should deal with the people and issues that are troubling them.

This month will bring you so much closer on an intimate level as well. Although Libra has so much empathy in February, do not allow yourself to become too drained in dealing with the problems of your partner and do not become directly involved. Single Libra may find that new love springs from a relationship of dependency i.e. where you are helping or supporting someone.

Money and Finance

A good month for financial analysis, for doing budgeting and for setting up my financial goals.

This is a really good month for crunching numbers and you should use some quiet time to settle down with a calculator and understand exactly what your incomings and outgoings are, and where there is scope for reduction.

If you need a better understanding of accounting or tax affairs, this is an excellent time to get advice. So if you had thought of employing an investment advisor, tax consultant or accountant, this is a great time to make a connection with someone who you can't rust and who can give valuable advice.

Living and Loving to the Full

This month enhancing love magic is all about making your love interest or partner feel special. Everyone wants to feel unique and this is strongly linked to feeling appreciated, but key to making a romance work is for each person to believe that their partner feels that they are special and the relationship is unique. So this is certainly a month for Libra showing your partner all the very special ways that you appreciate them and enjoy the relationship.

It is a certainly a time to focus on the positives: every single relationship has good and bad points, because nothing in life is perfect, but so often it's easy to perceive other people's relationships as perfect, and to focus on the flaws in one's own relationship. However this month, the challenge is to focus on all the beautiful positive and unique things about your relationship, to be grateful for them and a place far greater emphasis on those, rather than the problems.

Planetary Cautions

This month you need to avoid stress and overwork, it's very important for you to eat and drink in moderation and to get plenty of rest. This month you may be feeling slightly run down and depleted, so you may need to take additional supplements or vitamins and minerals, and make sure you're getting enough exercise and fresh air to replenish your body.

Work life balance is very important, you need to know how and when to switch off from work and particularly from clients and colleagues. Sometimes your clients and colleagues impinge on your personal space, so it's very important for you to have boundaries and to keep those boundaries strong.

You must avoid taking your problems home from work, because this can lead to a great deal of anxiety and worry that will simply not lead to more productivity or solving any problems.

Essence and Energies – "You won't know until you begin"

The essence this month is work, health and your underlying emotional connection to these.

This is a month time when you have to work on details and focus entirely on what you need to do to get the job done, or improve your health and this often means having to cut through distractions that draw you away from what's most important. It's all about economic use of time to get over the line, so that you have time for yourself.

It's vital to detect the psychological or emotional factors that drive certain attitudes to health and your daily job. Is work, or the actions of your colleagues draining your energy and affecting your motivation to eat well or exercise in a negative way? Are you attaching too much significance to work to fill an emotional gap? Are you allowing needy clients to attach to you? Or are you looking to clients and colleagues for succor and support.

This month is about understanding your attitudes to health and work and how they are connected to each other and alternatively to your emotional state. This can be essential to uncover or delve into before you set goals in connection with health improvement, as without understanding these connections, new health regimes may fail.

Affirmation: "I choose to have healthy relationships with colleagues and clients as this reflects a content emotions state that can enhance my diet and fitness aims.

Love and Romance

This month Libra can meet new people and make new friends, however often you can develop attachments to new friends very quickly and you may not be entirely sure of their motives or true personality.

This is not a good time to mix friendship and sex, it's also not a good time for you to have sexual relationships with professional colleagues or people you network with.

You tend to be in the mood for enjoying yourself and it's all too easy for you to get carried away in the moment i.e. at conferences, trade fairs or when travelling with colleagues. You need to exhibit a certain amount of self-discipline right now, because if you enter into casual relationships these can actually become a minefield of confused emotions and hurt, particularly for the other person, and it can end up souring good professional relationships.

Career and Aspiration

This is a good time for you to pursue individual projects or assignments, you work best when you can use your ingenuity and creativity without too much supervision or interference from authority.

Libra wants to conduct your work in your own inimitable way, and it's very important for you to stay true to your integrity and innate sense of justice when dealing with your clients and customers.

Frequently Libra wins the day this month by using your instincts, rather than going with the rules, as often merely following the rules ends up in a bad result for the very people you are trying to help. So when you go with your heart and you do what you feel is right, good things happen even if people in authority are not happy about it.

This is an energetic and creative time and you are full of imaginative energy and looking for opportunities to enjoy yourself. You are interested in entertaining and spreading goodwill. The problem is that you are very idealistic and can be blindsided by people with ulterior motives.

This is an ideal time to restart conversations or negotiations, pick up the phone, extend an olive branch and start reconciliations. This period can be very fertile for beginning new business partnerships and ventures.

Adventure and Motivation

This is a great time for Libra to organize activities, you may want to be at the center of organizing activities within your workplace to improve morale and spread Goodwill. On the other hand you may want to take the lead in terms of your social groups, to be the one who sets up events which everyone can look forward to and get excited about.

You are happiest this month when you are promoting harmony and fun, so any activity that you can do that helps generate a feel good factor and helps people to come together in a positive way, to either resolve differences or to celebrate achievements, is fantastic.

So the message is for you to throw a party, be social and help everyone to experience some good cheer.

Marriage and Family

With Venus and Jupiter in the solar 7th house, this is an excellent time for marriage, a good time for getting married and also for engagement.

Jupiter helps improve understanding and cooperation in relationships and even if your love life is rocky, this transit can pour oil over troubled waters. This is an ideal period to start marriage counselling or to use mediation to help settle an ongoing dispute. Legal problems can be smoothed over during this phase.

Relationships are important to you, however you may lack compassion by virtue of the fact that you are interested in good times rather than hard work. If your relationship is going well, that's excellent, however you can become impatient with a needy partner who isn't very upbeat or ready to party.

During this phase, you and your partner may get good news which will help increase prosperity. It may also be that you guys enjoy entertaining or hosting parties as a couple. You may become more social once again as a couple and element of fun and enjoyment re-enters your life.

Right now it is easier for you both to get your needs met and fulfilled in a relationship. There's a more relaxed atmosphere, you guys tend to be more laid-back and it's easier for you to leave your problems at the bedroom door and let your hair down to have fun.

So this month should be one of celebrating your relationship, relaxing, enjoying yourselves and possibly delaying any arguments or important decisions while you are in a fancy free frame of mind.

Money and Finance

This month you should avoid making too many outgoings to do with the purchases of luxuries for the home. This may not be a good month to shell out on any furniture or home entertainment systems, as they may be disappointing and in your heart it may not even be what you really want.

You often end up making bad financial decisions when you allow yourself to be persuaded by others or cajoled into things. It is important this month for you to stick with your budget and with your pre-existing plans, because it's all too easily easy for you to get persuaded into something, or to make purchases in the heat of the moment just to please other people, or get in the spirit of the moment.

Living and Loving to the Full

Key to love and romance right now is forgiveness and positivity, and you need to be totally willing to let go past grievances and to revel in the true meaning of forgiveness and letting go.

This is a time to look forward to the next chapter and to plan ahead with a totally generous and well-meaning mindset.

Nothing which you plan or discusses with your partner now should incorporate a degree of vengefulness or vendetta, you should focus on a fresh slate and you should be willing to give your partner a second chance. You should also be less critical of yourself and ensure that you are releasing guilt from the past and have achieved some sort of absolution, either through meditation or good communication with a partner.

All grievances should be forgot and never brought to mind.

Planetary Cautions

Libra craves recognition and you want to push yourself forward into situations where you think you are going to make an impression, but things are unlikely to turn out as you wish especially if you act out of character, or in a way which is in contrast to your usual persona. If you want to grab the headlines in your sphere of influence you must capitalize on your position or build on what you have rather than striking out in on unrelated tangent.

You are attracted to impossible relationships and yet you often need to feel as if these are meant to be. You may fall for people who cannot offer you much, but with whom you feel an odd kinship. However, you are displaying a vulnerable side of yourself and that can leave you open to needy people or people who want to take advantage, often these two combine in certain personality types.

Moon Magic

The new moon phase extends from the 21st of March to the 6th of April, this waxing phase is the perfect fortnight for new initiatives, setting plans, establishing goals, starting anything prospective and being proactive. This is the action phase, details below:

The waxing phase is excellent for marriage and improving relationships or committing to a lover. This is good for partnerships, business and personal. Teamwork and cooperation or conflict resolution is successful.

This is a good time for property development, house hunting and buying property. A good time for planning family events and entertaining. Favorable for pensions and savings planning.

New fitness routines and weight loss or dietary goals are not favored. Not a good time to join a gym. Delegating, recruitment and outsourcing can be problematic.

Dealing with money matters connected to loans, taxes and debt is not favored. A time to do research on financial matters to gain better clarity.

Sex counseling or better communication about sex is difficult. Not favorable for tax planning or taking on financial responsibility for others.

This is not a good time for major changes to your image or the way you go about business. You need to be careful of physical safety and in combat sports. It's important to look after your health and do everything in moderation.

Not favorable for totally new activities.

APRIL

Energies and Essence – "I got a new sensation
Mm, perfect moments
That's so impossible to refuse. "

This is a month for embracing change and adapting to fast-moving circumstances. Now Libra often like their comfort zones and while you are a very entrepreneurial, proactive sign and you can be someone who becomes set in your ways at times, and the challenge this month is for you to embrace circumstances that are likely to be a little bit unnerving, nerve-racking or which produce anxiety.

The reason you should embrace this dynamism is to move situations in your career or relationship forward. Move towards the challenges to get away from a comfort zones and tackle situations that you know need to be dealt with, which perhaps you have been putting off or trying to diplomatically avoid. It's time to take a more wholehearted, straightforward approach to certain hurdles, and be more fearless in the way you tackle them. So this is a month to embrace your courage and to get a spirit on.

Affirmation: "I enjoy the rush and challenge of change."

Love and Romance

Matters of the heart may have a life of their own, proving difficult to manage or fully understand and so you have to just wing it and enjoy the moment, without overthinking.

Whatever emotional hold previous relationships have on you, may become more than you can handle during this month, and circumstances may push you to make internal adjustments that can actually free you from this hold, which is great for new relationships going forward.

The key right now in relationships is thinking big and not believing anything is impossible, so often in relationships you are limited by your own perception of what is achievable and it's time to shift that boundary.

You will recognize that in order to move forward in love, you have to leave certain elements of your past behind. Pressure can build between the opportunities for new love and the force of ingrained patterns that may interfere with new relationships developing in a deeper fashion.

The saying, 'the only thing to fear is fear itself,' and that is the attitude that needs to be taken in your relationship. The only barrier is fear itself and the barriers that you create in your mind, the more you and your partner move forward with audacity and courage the more the relationship can be repaired and reach new levels of enjoyment and fulfilment.

Career and Aspiration

Mars in Cancer represents an excellent time for action and initiative in advancing your career. Your leadership abilities are enhanced and you benefits from greater decisiveness and guile.

You're quite strong willed and resists interference from authority and other powers that may not have your best interests at heart.

This is a great time for going for a promotion or job where there is a lot of competition for the position, as you're quite inspired when you goes head to head with fellow professionals or colleagues.

Leadership, activities involving mechanical assembly or innovation and jobs requiring physical exertion or a great deal of energy and fire are favored.

You may discover an opportunity to be more visible in your career and if you can manage your ego, you can initiate a project that involves construction, sports management or start a new business.

The focus this month is deep thinking and analyzing. It's important to get to the bottom of things, you should look at situations closely and examine the motives of other people, looking for hidden agendas.

While this is not a time to be paranoid or to look for issues where there are none, it's certainly a time for a greater awareness of all the different forces at play both in the family dynamic, at work all within your social life.

Adventure and Motivation

Libra is inspired to connect with your forceful and ambitious nature this month, situations tend to encourage you to be more assertive, less compromising and more spontaneous.

April is a dynamic time that can offer outstanding opportunities for adventure, new experiences advancement of your desires and achievement and you don't have to have a clear vision, because often just taking a chance on something new leads to a new vision emerging.

Libra can benefit from an increased intensity within yourself, or from others around you. This can serve to excite, inspire or mislead you and yet whatever happens, it's a great learning experience.

Marriage and Family

This month there is a powerful impetus for change in your marriage. New directions, new perspectives, new ideas and different goals are needed to take the marriage forward. Libra and your partner can feel a big change coming and yet vested interests and some emotional blocks are holding you both back.

There are some issues connected to the past that need to be resolved and you guys may want to talk about family and issues around the home that really require resolution and fixing, before you guys can truly fulfill your potential as a couple.

The strong bonds that are forged with family and community need work or else weakness there can jeopardize new pages in marriage. Libra can make an important new start in your marriage, but unless the family are on board or in the loop, it may not be as successful.

Any idealistic images about the domestic sphere that are unrealistic must be acknowledged.

Your hopes for happy times and special moments together may not meet your expectations, if you have not yet learned from and resolved the karma you have created together.

It's important for you and your partner to have open straightforward conversations, this is definitely a time where honesty and calling a spade a shovel works in relationships. It's time to move away from people pleasing, diplomacy and treading on eggshells and to roll up your sleeves and get done what needs to be done in order to make the relationship successful.

Money

This month Libra must be really cautious of being talked into spending or investing money.

You should carefully consider any advice you get and whether it's actually compatible with your innate nature. One man's meat is another man's poison and that is the best cliché to sum up this month.

It's easy for you to become inspired or get carried away, and often any repressed emotions or unresolved personal issues, can cloud your judgment.

It's best for you to stay detached and understand where emotions get the better of you in terms of judgment.

Living and Loving to the Full

In April, the way to improve the magic in love, is to experience novel things together in order to find the romance that you guys desire. Be willing to take risks, be bold and expand your vision of what's possible and you guys may end up finding excitement again. Single Libra may discover love in the most unlikely places, but the key is to be in those unlikely places.

This month has the potential to be the start of new journey in love, so it's time to place less emphasis on what's gone before and to look ahead.

Experiencing adrenaline and the thrill or trepidation of doing something new helps add a spark to love, especially when you are doing these new things together.

You should risk embarrassment or even rejection, because you may just find what you're looking for.

In love and relationships, you should be confident and have faith that all things will work out well.

Planetary Cautions

Mercury going retrograde on the 21st of April in Taurus means that any financial matters that you share or manage with others, or where you rely on the government are less reliable or harder to understand or control.

This is not a good time to take on more debt, borrow from family or start a new tax savings plan.

Passive income from donations, subscriptions and benefits could be interrupted or may experience delays.

You should also be careful of taking on more responsibility for others people's money and in jobs like accountant, financial planner or tax advisor you should be wary of any big new clients or any new demands from clients.

This is not a good time to start a career to do with bookkeeping, accounting, purser, treasurer or tax advisor.

New sexual relationships or sex counseling is not helpful during this phase.

Moon Magic

The new moon phase extends from the 20th of April to the 5th of May this waxing phase is the perfect fortnight for new initiatives, setting plans, establishing goals, starting anything prospective and being proactive. This is the action phase, details below:

The waxing phase is excellent for financial matters and investment in assets for your business. This is a good time for personal money management and making budgets. Investing in low risk assets is favored. Good for commitment and depth in relationship.

Group goals and networking or social media marketing is supercharged. Market research is important.

Another important period for new career directions, becoming self-employed or taking your destiny into your own hands. A time to be proactive.

Mercury retrograde in Taurus on 21st means that a certain amount of caution is needed in terms of new sexual and intimate relationships. Not favorable for arranging loans and finances. Tax planning and claiming rebates or insurance payouts is tricky. Debt and financial matters where you rely on others is more contentious.

Sexual understanding and better intimate communication in relationships is to be strived for.

Energies and Essence – "There were nights of endless pleasure It was more than any laws allow, maybe baby!"

This month the theme is sexual and intimate satisfaction.

It's very important for you to focus on sexual matters between you and your partner, but this isn't just the sex life, it's also intimacy. Couples who begin to drift apart in terms of intimate sharing, being affectionate with each other and being playful with each other even if it doesn't always result in sex, drift apart in other ways too.

Having a good sexual relationship and being able to relate to your partner intimately is the gateway to deep emotional understanding. In May, trust and ability to let go and enjoy each other in the bedroom means that in other aspects of life, it's much easier for you to exchange emotionally and interact in a meaningful spiritual way.

This is an important time for you to assess the kind of boundaries and walls that may exist between you and your partner i.e. the secrets, the things that you refuse to share, the things that you are wary of about your partner and to ask where have these come from, how long have they been there and how can you tackle them these.

There are unspoken rules in all relationships, but why is this? This is the time for you to maybe broach these taboos, tackle them and change them.

Affirmation: "Rules are made to be broken and I'm breaking all the bad rules I set myself in relationships."

Love and Romance

This is an excellent month for love, and something rather important could be about to develop that can become very passionate. However a romance that begins this month is just a seed, it's going to grow into something more substantial and tangible with time. So often there are opportunities to meet new people, or to go different places and you should definitely grab those and make the most of it because there's certainly the potential for some surprises in terms of love, and the possibility to connect with someone who may at first become a friend or colleague, but who in the next few months becomes far more than that.

Part of this month in love is breaking taboos, very often we stop communicating once we get into a steady relationship because we think we know all there is to know, but that's never the case, people are dynamic and therefore relationships have to evolve but they can't evolve without conversation.

This is a month for you and your partner to have discussions about where you are both at in the relationship, where you see things going, how you're going to get there and what you are both happy or unhappy about.

Career and Aspiration

This is a tricky month for Libra, because Libra has an inner conflict between wanting to lead, but your nature at heart is being a very co-operative person, who likes to be a team player. This month you want to enjoy the vibe you get from group activities or working with others, but you really don't like having to co-operate with others, because you're quite impatient, eager to manage everything and you don't like to hang around waiting for other people to make their mind up, because you tend to be quite decisive this month.

You're ideally placed where you can work in a team who are looking for a leader, and who are therefore going to want to submit to your power, and enjoy the fact that you're providing direction. This is not a good time for you to be vying for control with a group of other stubborn or strong willed individuals as this can lead to a lot of frustration and not much progress.

This is not necessarily an easy month to work with, or co-ordinate artistic and creative people, because these people tend to be quite precious and tempers flare.

Adventure and Motivation

This is a month when you may have an A-Ha moment where you feel you can break through previous barriers. This could be to do with any activity that you feel has been in the doldrums in your life, so it could be your romantic life, your career or your hobbies, but at the moment a wave of inspiration hits and you're suddenly more motivated about pursuing your ideas and particularly your passions.

It's time to look past the hurdles, to see the vision again clearly and open your eyes to a new world of possibility. You have a lot of creative potential at the moment and are driven by a strong force and a desire to access that potential, so this is an excellent time for any creative venture, or also for any project where you're working on a particular invention or idea that you think could be useful to both yourself or others.

An unexpected event may provide the catalyst externally, but if you are honest you will admit that you were already restless and dying for change. You tend to have faith that things will work out and that makes you quite bold, you attract a fair bit of luck and initially at least, your new ways of doing thing pay off. There is a danger that many of the new projects and activities you initiate have such a successful start and get off to such a flyer that potential pitfalls and dangers are not immediately apparent and can form a spoke in the wheels later on.

Marriage and Family

This is definitely a month where married Libra needs to embrace change, and especially changes that rock the boat. Routine is killing the relationship and the passion right now. Libra needs to recognize all the ways you and your partner are actually in bondage to stale old routines and ideas. Maybe you are both becoming slaves to your worries or working too hard and not spending enough time together.

This is an excellent month for date nights, maybe going to a concert together or doing something that you used to do when you were dating in order to reignite the energy and excitement in your relationship. It's almost like there's a well of sexual energy and chemistry between you that is not being tapped into. Perhaps you guys aren't allowing yourselves time to get into the right kind of mood, so this month you need to be doing leisure and fun activities that really help you get into not only a romantic frame of mind, but a passionate mood.

In all relationships it's important to embrace individuality, encourage your partner's individuality and freedom and make sure that you're self-expression and individuality is also fostered in the relationship. Often relationships become controlling and restrictive because one partner starts feeling insecure and then resorts too controlling tactics to shut the other partner down.

The insecurity usually comes from a lack of self-esteem and the ability to express, that's why in order to stop controlling behavior on either of your parts, the first key is encouraging each other to express themselves fully and frequently. Then after that, getting rid of relationship rules or rituals that are stale for one or both of you, and reviewing the whole way the relationship works to be sure that there is no bad feeling.

Money and Finance

In terms of money, this is a very important month. I've already said that any activity where you need to work with others, or you rely on others for money can be quite unpredictable. However, aspects of your money where you have total control, can deliver some excellent results this month. Effort and good communication lead to results.

If you need to make ends meet, the way to do it is through streamlining and using new technology to save time. You should either research, or invest in new computer programs or equipment that will be labor-saving, and will free up time which you can use to put directly into money making activities or more productive pursuits.

Living and Loving to the Full

In terms of love and romance, this is a month when Libra should just go for broke, you should be very active about creating romance and being spontaneous in the relationship sphere. You need to act on your inspiration and not be too self-controlled or bound by what you perceives as your partner's expectations.

This is a good time to think out the box in love, if there's anything that you have had on your mind or that you're been wanting to say or do with your partner, and you're been deliberating, you should come right out with it and say it. No more holding back. This is a phase when doing something out the box really works in love, and so you should listen to your instincts, follow your whims and breathe some excitement into the relationship.

Planetary Cautions

Mercury continues to be in Taurus and it is retrograde until the 15th and thus until the 15th, you should still be very cautious of anything to do with debt, borrowing or loans, this is also not a good time to invest money in a business partnership.

New accounting and tax activities conducted for your own business or on behalf of someone else are not favored until that time.

The retrograde time is an excellent time for in-depth research, analysis or auditing.

This is also a time where you must remember to keep secrets, because confidentiality and integrity is very important, so you must be discreet.

After the 15th all your accounting and borrowing activities can proceed again, as well as discussions with your partner about money and sex.

Moon Magic

The new moon phase extends from the 19th of May to the 3rd of June this waxing phase is the perfect fortnight for new initiatives, setting plans, establishing goals, starting anything prospective and being proactive. This is the action phase, details below:

This is not a good waxing phase for dealing with large government departments and corporations. Solitary work is less satisfying. Meditation and holistic pursuits or retreats are not satisfying or successful.

The waxing period is not favorable for long haul trips, publishing or promotion. Not a good time for new academic goals. New international trade is not successful. Cross cultural romance is not advisable.

This period is excellent for new romance, dating and social events. Business related to entertainment and leisure is successful. A good time for matters related to children. Creative and artistic ventures and competitive activities in connection with sports are successful.

New IT projects, launching websites and mass communication is not successful. Not great for exams or public speaking. Internet dating and dating apps are not favored.

JUNE

Essence and Energies – "Like a virgin."

This month the energies are all about your desire to re-discover a sense of meaning, purpose and inspiration in your life.

Not only is this a good time to make changes, it's also a fantastic time to try new activities or to do something for the first time, which gives you a sense of excitement which can re-energize you emotionally.

We all need excitement and the stimulation of change in our life, but often they are so many obligations and pressures that it's easy to slip into routines that ultimately suck the life out of us and make us rather lackluster and uninspired.

So the key this month is seeking your inner star and allowing yourself to shine, so make it your goal to pursue a new course of action that will make you excited, put a spring in your step and bring you in contact with people who also feel inspired and positive so that you can build up a momentum of positivity and fresh perspective.

Affirmation: "I reach into myself and draw on my inner magic."

Love and Romance

Whether you are looking for love or in a stable relationship, this is a time of happiness, not because everything is necessarily going perfectly, but because there is the expectation of positive change and you feel that things are moving in the right direction, and this gives you a lot of inspiration.

This is an excellent time to meet someone new, the more you have been through a personal transformation and have understood the type of person you are and who exactly you need, the more you will attract the most successful relationship. This is a wonderful time for meeting someone with whom you will share excellent chemistry and a wonderful spiritual bond.

However if you have not yet fully understood what you are looking for in a relationship, what your personality type is and who ultimately would suit you, this is an excellent time to work on that. You may want to do some meditations or reading, some psychological study or anything that helps you get a better sense of where you are at and who is suitable. If you do this, it can be wonderful time for romance. Sometimes in romance we are groveling around in the dark, but we don't need to be, because by simply working on our self-understanding, our personality and patterns, our relationship themes etc., we can begin to work out immediately who's right and who is wrong and this can be invaluable.

Career and Aspiration

This month it's important for you in your career not to try and run before you can walk, there's a sense of heightened expectation and wanting to bite off more than you can chew.

Sticking to plans and staying within the guidelines you've already set yourself is important, there's a temptation to get carried away in the moment, and to rush on tangents and these can land up being quite expensive.

You should also be careful not to over promise or raise expectations of either clients, customers or the people you works with. It's very important to level with people and be honest with yourself about the pros and cons and the potential pitfalls of any plans.

So while this is a great month for expansion and being positive, you really must make sure you covers the downside and you don't become blind to potential problems, as when these occur it's going to be very frustrating for you.

This could be an excellent time to spearhead a networking project, a consciousness or awareness raising project or something that helps you unite with people get something off the ground and do something that you feel will have a lasting impact that is positive.

Adventure and Motivation

This month is an ideal time for you to express yourself, it could be in terms of creativity, romantically or in a sporting sense, but you should certainly do things that are different from your normal routine.

It's vital for you to experience a certain kind of freedom in your life, so while relationships, teamwork and collaborating with colleagues is important to you, you still need a space where you can be totally indulgent and spontaneous, without being tied to the needs of others.

So in terms of adventure and fun this month, you need to feed the playful and whimsical side of yourself by doing quirky and eccentric things, which may make no sense to others, without feeling the need to apologize for this or explain yourself.

Marriage and Family

The key in successful marriage this month, is for Libra to show you have the heart of a lion, so you should be courageous and magnanimous, which means you must be willing to step up and apologize, if need be, but at the same time you must be totally willing to make amends and to show your partner, in a hole hearted way, your feelings. It is certainly time to be more affectionate, but in a caring way, not necessarily just as a way that seeks to stimulate passion.

It's important for you to be more proactive in terms of the children, which could be disciplining the children if they are younger, or communicating and guiding children who are older. It's time for you to show a good example and also to be the cool head that's needed to regulate family relationships, and in some cases mediate between the children or different family members.

This is a wonderful time of year for couples who have been together for a long time to try new things to stimulate your sex life whether it be by adding props, with role play, reading erotic literature or simply having more time when you can simply be with each other in a relaxed way rather than just falling into bed exhausted.

Money

This is generally a positive month for income, you may experience an increase in sales or have a small rise in your pay packet.

Situations in wider society and the economic world tend to play in your favor and this results in some positive news regarding money.

What's good about this month, is that you can make substantial savings if you shop around, so it's very important for you to listen to word on the grapevine, keep an eye on certain forums, or listen for signals in your network of discounts or opportunities to buy some new assets at cheaper prices.

This month it pays to be in the loop, so you need to make sure you are utilizing to the max any subscriptions to trade magazines, journals or newspapers so you gets the full benefit of information, because this can save you money.

Living and Loving to the Full

This month the way Libra can enhance relationships is by showing strength of character, being direct and forthright. So what you don't want to be doing is beating around the bush or showing your partner that you are obfuscating or making excuses, because all these sow seeds of doubt in your partner's mind.

Most people prefer the truth and want to hear it straight, and therefore it is important for Libra to acknowledge that, and try not to hide behind words diplomacy or meaningless gestures.

This month the advice is saying what you mean, meaning what you say and giving compliments, but also not being scared to wade into difficult conversations. You should broach any issues in an adult and alpha fashion, with a positive motivation behind starting conversations, aimed at fostering better understanding or facilitating change.

Planetary Cautions

This month it's important for you to avoid jumping to conclusions, you can be very impatient and sometimes you want to preempt things by assuming you knows the details, and acting on that assumption, rather than waiting to find out the actual details.

Right now you need to consider more clearly how you interact with other people, and the effect your actions have in terms of a domino effect on the wider world.

Often what you do now has unintended consequences and that's why I say you need to consider the domino effect. Your restlessness mean you're impatient to get things done but you don't always think of the potential for fallout.

Moon Magic

The new moon phase extends from the 18th of June to the 2nd of July. This waxing phase is the perfect fortnight for new initiatives, setting plans, establishing goals, starting anything prospective and being proactive. This is the action phase, details below:

This is not the best phase for spearheading networks, particularly professional networks and coming up with new radical ideas. Not a good period for friends with benefits arrangements. Joining political movements is not advisable. Attending large group gatherings is not favored.

Ideal for academic goals and further education. Great for renewed excitement and adventure in life. Perfect for planning business expansion to new geographical areas, advertising, promotion and publishing. Suits teaching and spreading ideas.

Marriage and engagement are not favored. This is not a suitable time to commit in love. Not the best time for negotiations, new business partnerships or beginning a legal claim. Not suitable for new sexual relationships.

Large scale financial matters, new joint investment and taking on debt is not favored. Psychological counseling may not be successful.

This may not be a great zone for romance, creative affairs and businesses connected to entertainment and leisure. This is also not a good month for activities related to children, both personal and business.

Property and real estate matters are favored. A good time for large family events, entertaining and celebrations. Renovations and adaptation of the home is favored. Great for business involving catering, hospitality and the environment.

Essence and Energies – "What a joy, what a life, what a chance"

This month is important for you to define yourself in terms of how you project to the outside world.

Your identity is paramount, and you may find the energy this month helps you to shape it in meaningful ways. You are able to increase your personal power this month, both materially and in self-awareness, but there is usually is something that you have to give up or leave behind in order to truly come into your own.

It could be that certain strong attachments of the past have less influence over you, especially if they are in the way of a deeper realization of who you are, which is an important hallmark of this July. You may initially struggle to let go of what you used to believe and this is essential, although it can be difficult because these attachments are comfortable, but in the midst of this period you must recognize that what you give up now, allows for the emergence of what is likely more satisfying going forward.

Affirmation: "I continue to grow and old patterns and attachments cannot confine or define me continually."

Love and Romance

With Venus retrograde, this is definitely not a good time for friends-with-benefits relationships, or developing feelings with colleagues, or while you're at a conference.

Not only is Venus retrograde, but Mars the ruler of your solar 7th house is in the 12th house, so it's really important in romance to be discreet, compassionate and careful.

There's quite a strong desire for relationships that are a little bit risky, that require secrecy or that involve some sort of shenanigans, so Libra must be careful.

Love and romance in July can be a Pandora's box, things are often more complicated than they first seemed, and that's why you need to be really clear about who and what you are getting into when you initiates romance. Right now it's quite an odd environment and they are many thorny issues in new relationships, so you need to be aware of it.

For single Libra, it's probably best for you to stay single and enjoy doing things which create value in terms of your self-worth and allow you to experience the benefits of your own creativity and individuality.

Career and Aspiration

This month communication and using debating and presentation skills are very important. This may be a month where you are a lot more visible within your career, attention falls onto you as well as scrutiny, and you have to be sure that you are precise, succinct and that you know your onions.

You may be more likely to have to give speeches, present proposals or undergo an assessment, but this is an excellent month for you to gain the attention of important people and increase your profile.

This may also be a good time to redo your business website or update all your online profiles so that you attract the attention of new clients, or possibly are headhunted.

There are opportunities to do interviews, write articles or present to an audience.

An excellent time to teach and also spread ideas, so if you have a message, you should focus on that.

Adventure and Motivation

This month you have a strong desire to re-discover a sense of meaning in your life, so it's important for you to follow activities which inspire you or give you purpose. Libra is not usually the sort of person who keeps doing something out of a sense of obligation, but right now is the time for you to analyze how you spend your time, and how much of it is spent doing things in your spare time that are actually contributing to your personal development.

Libra is going through an important internal process, you are shedding the old you and embracing a whole new you, and this will bring fresh perspectives in your life. However this also means that you have to devote time to new activities which truly replenish and fulfill you, and that means understanding which activities are superfluous or no longer relevant in your life, and getting rid of them.

You have a larger degree of patience for longer term goals which helps you to achieve success in these. You operate with consistency and enjoy taking responsibility. This month's transit are terrific help if you have to be systematic and methodical in your work.

Don't force the pace, know the limits or each situation, but wait for the wave and catch it because things always come around.

Courting the opinion of others is not the way to go; have faith in your ideas no matter how they are received. You may have to proceed alone in the short run until others come around to your way of thinking, but is that not what leadership is all about and Libra are leaders.

Be an influencer and don't be afraid to back yourself and keep the faith with your ideas until they are proven valuable. Once again be patient, keep the "you wait and see" smugness to yourself or you will succumb to the arrogance.

Marriage and Family

Marriage is strengthened this month if you and your partner understand the spiritual journey you guys are on together, rather than seeing everything as a procession of days or series of routines and commitments. It may be a good time for you and your partner to consider what they have achieved, how far they have come, the obstacles they have overcome and how this has brought them closer together.

So often the hardships, difficulties and struggles in life tear couples apart, but they can be a uniting force if couples understand them with a higher spiritual awareness, and see these challenges as a way to grow as people, to become more humble, more compassionate and more loving. When seen in this context, the struggles can bring couples closer together in wisdom and understanding, rather than tearing them apart.

For those you love, you need to be a rock to them: devoted, practical and solid in their time of need. A partner or family member will look to you for advice more than ever due to your keen insight and inner self-assurance. Your balance of wisdom and keen perception will mean that you get some key decisions bang on – woe betide those who ignore your advice or go against you.

A month for maturity where you will take a step back and look at where you are in relationships: a mini audit you may say. Realism will triumph over idealism when it comes to goals and plans for the relationship. Things will come to a head, your strength of character may be tested too, but your unique talents and abilities will be recognized. Libra rise to the challenge without fail in love!

Money and Finance

This month the message in money is to be ready for anything. You should make sure that you have sufficient cash and are also not overstretched. This month there can be surprising events and shocks in the outer economy, so you need to ensure that you are ready for anything and have maximum flexibility.

Fate demands that you keeps moving, growing and increasing your understanding, and that's why anything that you used to rely on, which is now outdated, outworn or was holding you back, will have to go. So you should be ready to embrace a lot of new ideas, new technology and new ways of thinking in your business.

Living and Loving to the Full

This month the key to enhancing love relationships and marriage begins within. This is the month where Libra really do need to address your shadow self, any repressed emotions regarding envy, revenge, hatred or anger need to be expelled.

It's very important to understand projection, very often the emotions that you suppresses by being diplomatic, people pleasing or conflict avoiding end up erupting in another part of your life. Often your partner acts out these emotions subconsciously, or maybe they erupt through unexpected events or family arguments.

So it's very important for you to own your frustrations, your angers, hatred etc. and to begin to work on them honestly, in private by yourself, and these will be much less likely to disrupt your relationship in unpleasant ways.

Planetary Cautions

This month Venus, which is your chart ruler goes retrograde in Leo. This means that it's important for you to avoid large group activities, and new networking initiatives are not necessarily favored

You need to ply energy into the things that you are already involved in, this is not a time to be opening up any brand new activities, particularly social activities.

Often people are very demanding of you, friends, family and acquaintances can be needier in terms of seeking your advice or your support. So you need to have strong boundaries, in many ways you need a certain amount of privacy this month, that's why you don't want to spread yourself too thin on the social scene, both at work and at home.

Moon Magic

The new moon phase extends from the 17th of July to the 30th of July. This waxing phase is the perfect fortnight for new initiatives, setting plans, establishing goals, starting anything prospective and being proactive. This is the action phase, details below:

The waxing phase is not a great time for political matters or activism. A time to be an individual and not follow the crowd. Not a good period to be controversial. New legislation should be analyzed for how it influences your business. Networking is not favored.

Not a successful time for new business ventures in hospitality, tourism or catering. Working from home is not ideal. Real estate and home improvements are not favored. Large scale family events and having family to stay is not advisable.

This is a great period for your finances, cash flow improves. It's a positive months for investing, buying new assets and gaining new clients. A good month for financial analysis and changes.

Energies and Essence – "You can't start a fire
You can't start a fire without a spark"

With your ruler Venus going retrograde in Leo, you are on the horns of many dilemmas and you are challenged not to live in denial. The first thing to do is to step into your own power by being willing to accept the consequences of your actions and to also acknowledge the extent to which your partner or significant people in your life accepts responsibility for their actions.

Don't hide from your guilt, acknowledge your mistakes, own them and make amends. You must understand that your actions that are in the past, are not necessarily a reflection of who you are now, or they don't have to be.

Your future depends on your actions today - and so what can you do to tip the scales in favor of your own progress. How can you make up for your wrongs? Taking action gives you a chance to evolve and end energy sapping self-judgment.

Remember not to be dragged down by people who can't move on from their own mistakes or resolve their issues.

Making decisions is easier when you eliminate guilt and self-recriminations.

Affirmations: "The future is happening now and I act decisively."

Love and Romance

Although this is still not the best time for double dating, social occasions and cyber dating or internet dating, it's still a good time to be mingling with people, creating new friendships and expanding your social circles because right now there's a lot going on behind the scenes, and a potential new relationship could be developing, even if you haven't identified it as such right yet.

Someone you already know within a work context has probably got an interest in you, and yet you may be so busy looking elsewhere you haven't actually noticed.

So while there are important seeds developing in love, a full connection has not yet been established, but it will soon reveal itself, so the key is for you to be patient, to keep your eyes open and to keep putting your best foot forward in all your social relationships.

Success in love is about being truly open and unless you are, you can't truly appreciate the opportunities. This isn't the time to be looking for someone absolutely perfect, perfection itself is an illusion and only exists when you are infatuated. True love is understanding the emotional potential inherent in a relationship and how much you and another complement each other. Looking for perfection leads to a lack of diversity of ability in a relationship as it sets the field too narrowly.

Career and Aspiration

In career this is an action orientated time, but it's also quite practical and grounded. This is an excellent time for you to identify opportunities where you can expand your business, use your talents more successfully or achieve financial success by doing something before anybody else does.

This month it is important for you to be entrepreneurial, identify gaps in the market or openings before other people and to rush in and take advantage.

Once again it's important for you to be abreast of new information, the news and new technology and attending trade fairs, conferences or seminars where cutting-edge information is discussed, can also be very helpful.

This is a good time for start-up businesses or for Libras who work with people in start-up businesses, you're quite energized in terms of your business potential and ambition and that is a good thing.

Adventure and Motivation

The terrific thing about this month is that you become more aware of your own strength and if you make that courageous first move, suddenly the spirit is with you and you begin to do and say things you never knew you were capable of and suddenly you are gaining influence and making strides. It's all about gathering yourself, understanding the forces against you.

You can provide leadership on critical matters in your personal life or profession life right now. Difficult decisions can be made during this transit and it's a perfect time to use your influence by being diplomatic and using strong powers of persuasion, however direct conflict is not a good idea.

Marriage and Family

This is a time of intense negotiation in marriage, it's a time where you and your partner need to set aside time to have important debates or to discuss problems, and how to solve them or move things forward.

This is definitely a time when you have to be a good listener, you have to sincerely try to understand your partner's point of view, their priorities and their needs, and then you have to show that you are incorporating those in terms of the decision making.

It's all too easy now for you to assume you know your partner well and to second guess them, but things are changing right now, your partner may surprise you with some of their current opinions or desires, and so it's very important for these conversations to take place and for you to check with your partner before making any decisions.

You cannot play lip service to your partner's feelings, that won't cut it.

This a certainly a time to work on understanding in relationships. Forgiveness is always important in love, but forgiveness shouldn't mean allowing repeat offending. Don't be conned by charm and kind words, look for actions and a genuine attempt to take responsibility and make amends.

Money and Finance

This is generally a positive month for money, there may be good things in the offing but you may not have experienced the cash flow yet. It could well be that you know a pay rise is not far off, or a new job with increased prospects is coming, or you may know that some new clients with greater potential are showing an interest.

You may receive a lot of positive information that leads you to believe that your finances will soon be on the up, and they will be, but this hasn't manifested yet so you just need to be careful to groom all these opportunities so that they bear fruit.

Living and Loving to the Full

This is an excellent time for Libra and your partner if you work together in business, or if you are thinking of setting up a business together. This may even be a good time to combine your finances, open a new joint bank account or purchase something of significance together.

So if Libra is in an established relationship, but you guys haven't committed yet, this maybe the time to start sharing a flat, or sharing a pet or beginning to share something important as a gateway to moving the relationship to the next level.

Sharing isn't a small thing, it's very important, so the more Libra wants to share, with either your wife/hubbie or your partner, secrets, personal anecdotes or possessions that are important you, the more it says that the relationship is getting serious.

Planetary Cautions

Venus is in retrograde this month, so it's still a time of caution in terms of new relationships, sexual relationships and brand new activities. This is also a time for you to be careful of your health and sugar intake. You could feel more indulgent at this time, you're more likely to resort to negative ways of fulfilling emotional needs like eating or spending.

The challenge this month is for you to find positive ways to feel good, and often this is linked to you regaining your individualism. So any activity that you can get involved in where you can use your unique creative skills and talents and have a sense of personal achievement are very important.

So this month, personal satisfaction through personal achievement are to be striven for. It's a less good month for you doing activities in a team or where you have to share the limelight.

Moon Magic

The new moon phase extends from the 16th of August to the 30th of August. This waxing phase is the perfect fortnight for new initiatives, setting plans, establishing goals, starting anything prospective and being proactive. This is the action phase, details below:

This is a great time for goals involving groups and travelling with groups of people. Networking is successful. With Venus still retrograde you must be careful of new associates, you're better off building stronger relationships with existing colleagues rather than branching into totally new territory.

Career goals, leadership and new career directions are favored. A suitable time to expand your business and use new management techniques. PR and public speaking or more high profile activities are successful.

This is a great period for your finances, cash flow improves. It's a positive months for investing, buying new assets and gaining new clients. A good month for financial analysis and changes.

This is a great time for teaching, academic studies and also publishing. Long distance travel and international business relations are favored, relations with the in-laws can be improved.

This is an excellent time for romance, brand new relationships, dating and social occasions. A good time for planning entertainment and leisure activities for personal enjoyment or business, and an ideal time to work with children.

A time to be cautious in health or with medication. Not a great time to start new diet or join a gym.

This is an excellent time for being more assertive and competitive physical activity and sports are favored. While you should be careful in travel and combat sports, this is generally a good time for leadership and for new personal challenges involving fitness and your appearance.

Venus is still retrograde indicating an important time for resolving misunderstandings with friends.

SEPTEMBER

Essence and Energies – "Spirit to take a chance"

The essence this month is using your passion. A huge amount of success and personal achievement is possible especially if you pursue an activity which you have a passion for. It's time to devote energy to things that are emotionally involving, that hold significance and which you are proud to talk through others amount. It's important to understand what moves you, you need to engage in things that matter, that you control and that allow you a sense of satisfaction.

During this month transits tend to augment the motivating, excitable forces of your personality. It's not only about constructive action this month, it's also an excellent time to tear down what is predictable, limiting or dull in your life. Often to go chasing after things that you are passionate about requires that you purge whatever is a hindrance to getting this emotional satisfaction.

It's not necessarily easy to identify your passion, but you will feel a certain restlessness this month that at least encourages you to address any emptiness inside. Feeling like something is missing and your path is not the way you have expected it, is the cue to understanding the need for passion, something that drive a spark of excitement and meaning. Once you acknowledge what's missing, you can look to fill that void.

Affirmation: "I am ready to make space in my life for activities which are emotionally enjoyable and which excite me at a fundamental level."

Love and Romance

This month matters of the heart are quite confusing. Libra is very busy, you may be abrupt and when you're free, you could want to spend time alone or with large groups rather than with your new partner specifically. Bottom line is it's really hard to get your attention this month.

You can be a little too impersonal in close relationships, so a partner may feel you're a little cold, but you're merely distracted and your energy is quite scattered. You can be a little selfish this month. You're unlikely to want to commit even if you're in love, so it's best for a partner not to read too much into your behavior. Your goals this month and often distract you from love.

In new love, you'll need to embrace different things in order to find romance which is fulfilling, so be willing to take risks, be daring and expand your vision of the world and you may end up finding love in the most unlikely places. Surprises are part and parcel of the process.

Fear of rejection, should not hold you back, because if you open yourself up to the world, even with the risk of embarrassment or rejection, you may just find a rare gem of a romantic opportunity.

Career and Aspiration

With Mars in Libra you have a great deal of energy and you are able to get your stuff together and spearhead activities, be entrepreneurial and competitive. Mars can help you to be assertive and to tackle brand new activities that are usually intimidating or a little too combative for your nature.

However with Jupiter retrograde in Taurus and Mercury in Virgo retrograde, you are inspired by non-material and spiritual goals and so you may use your energy this month to pursue goals that are artistic, humanitarian or alternative.

This is an excellent time for working on goals that are slightly left of center or unorthodox. You may want to be a spokesperson for a cause or to rally large group of people in an effort that's got a social or political cause.

So you experience a lively energy this month and that will inspire you to do things that are quite surprising and spontaneous, but which also represents a higher purpose or calling.

You're very competitive and have a desire to win, be first and be the best in whatever you're doing, and this helps you make great strides this month in your career or in advancing your business interests.

Adventure and Motivation

Physical exertion or competitive activities are a fabulous outlet for your heightened energy, but you should be a little cautious if accidents or injuries, so you must warm up properly.

This month you're rather excited as many of your hopes and dreams feel more accessible and this brings a burst of positivity that feeds into a dynamic energy.

Group activities, attending large-scale events with lots of people, social gatherings or becoming more involved in activism are rewarding and life affirming activities.

It's also a great time for you to raise money or awareness for your favorite causes or charities.

Organizing events aimed at fund raising can be very satisfying.

Marriage and Family

Your personal interactions are highly charged and you're very persuasive. You're more effective in relationships because you're extremely direct and intense in your approach.

Relationships are subtly changing as you're got a more flexible perception of yourself making you emotionally more elusive during this month. You're decisive, but your actions are often out of character giving your partner pause for thought.

During this month relationships tend to be complicated and tricky, you often have to dig deep and work on improving understanding of your own psychology and the dynamics of the relationship to ensure that the relationship survives and thrives. This is a very important time in your life in which to be honest with yourself, to tackle your demons and to work on yourself.

Often encounters with other people (these may be in your relationships or your business relationships) are extremely intense and quite draining. You may need more time and space by yourself simply because relationships in general or an area where there is more contention and effort required to maintain harmony.

The boundaries that have defined the relationship up until now may dissolve or become less rigid. Fortunately there is much to gain from this, but if your partner likes predictability, they can experience a loss of control and may feel a little insecure or at sea.

You want to be freer now, with less encumbrances and you won't let responsibilities rule your life to the extent they did in the past.

You're following the truth of your heart rather than what others think is right.

Money and Finance

You're often good at managing money or helping raise money for others rather than for your own benefit. You may also be selected to manage money on behalf of a group or organization.

Money can flow from activities involving the avant-garde, new age, political blogging, or new scientific discovery.

Friends may help you to identify new money making opportunities, new jobs or different ways to generate income.

This is another good month to set things in place that will lead to greater income down the line, this includes networking or applying for government contracts.

Living and Loving to the Full

This month Libra can be romantic and free spirited about love, the best relationships are ones where you and a partner support each other's individuality, enjoy similar activities and have similar goals.

Couples who unite in causes bigger than themselves and who enjoy group or charitable events together thrive.

Being easy going and going with the flow rather than seeking to plan and manage everything leads to magic flowing in love.

Friendship is vital in relationships and so to enhance the magic, Libra and your partner must renew the friendship and camaraderie.

Have fun and be fancy free, don't seek control in relationships and allow things to happen organically and love explodes

Planetary Cautions

You should avoid acidic and highly spicy food. You need to spend time over meals rather than racing food down on the go. Fresh food, leafy greens and less highly processed foods are essential.

You must try to contain your high levels of enthusiasm and impatience, but being more aware of how people around you are feeling.

While you have good energy, and are enthusiastic about fitness goals, you do need to look after your health through a sensible balance of exercise and exertion with rest, plenty of sleep and water. In fact drinking enough water is vital. Libra often don't drink enough quality water and so this month your goal is water water water.

It's also important for you to be holistic about health and you must pay attention to your attitudes, your psychology as well as what you eat and when you eat it.

Moon Magic

The new moon phase extends from the 14th of September to the 29th of September. This waxing phase is the perfect fortnight for new initiatives, setting plans, establishing goals, starting anything prospective and being proactive. This is the action phase, details below:

This time the waxing period is tricky for major career change, PR and leadership. It's not ideal for corporate entertainment and public speaking or teaching.

This is an excellent day for highly competitive activity and sports, a very good time for leadership, being assertive, standing up for yourself and making a good impression.

A great time for positive change in attitudes.

Short distance travel, study, exams, presentations and internet dating are favored. An excellent time to follow through with all your communication goals with gusto, good for negotiation and new contracts. Communication speeds up but this is an excellent time for debate, a good period for quickly learning and mastering skills.

Energies and Essence – "Open your eyes and look at the day You'll see things in a different way"

This is a period when it's important for you to use your communication skills. You are more alert, observant and mentally sharp and it gives you a great boost of confidence to hold the floor, to express yourself verbally and have conversations with new people.

This is a time when you are very conscious of your purpose and you are able to project that clearly to others, you will put a lot of energy into communicating with people, but remember to be a good listener and not to be too subjective.

You should use this time to make an impression on other people and to debate, and you should not be deterred by any opposition even if it's fierce, because you can stand up for yourself, argue your corner, make your point and be heard, and this will contribute greatly to your self-esteem.

Affirmation: "As a Libran I am articulate and persuasive and I choose to communicate with confidence."

Love and Romance

If you are in a relationship where you feel you have run out of options, this month may bring about a breaking away from a relationship with a domineering partner, or a co-dependent relationship that was not allowing you to express your true nature.

You may suddenly recognize that the bonds that connect you to a partner may not be very healthy or supportive, so you may be better served by continuing to nurture your own independence and be proud of your individual path.

However, if you're in a really good relationship with deep spiritual understanding and where you and your partner are on a path of self-awareness, things can get more intense and the level of satisfaction is heightened even if there are some bones of contention or disputes.

This is not the best time to enter a new relationship because you can easily become infatuated and some of your attitudes may be slightly unrealistic, which can cause disappointments and problems later on.

Career and Aspiration

This is quite a hectic month and one where new information is coming at you and you have to understand what is important and what's not.

Libra will enjoy this fast paced month as it's full of the intellectual stimulation and social activities you thrive on.

You have an opportunity to express your ideas and communicate successfully to others which can impress clients and help you profit from your intelligence in terms of your ability to formulate and distribute information.

It's a great time for research and finding information important to your progress, it's also a perfect time for multi-tasking and jumping into many different things to gain experience or organize and manage your business.

You may have opportunities to give talks, interact with the public, meet new colleagues or have a chance to publicize your thoughts through writing or broadcasting.

Adventure and Motivation

Libra can learn a great deal about yourself this month sometimes via encountering some resistance, but you are not fearful, you are very brave and feel divinely protected. When you come face to face with aspects of yourself which are not desirable, you can deal with this honestly. Some experiences will humble you, but these are very important for you to discover a new place for yourself in society.

You may seek spiritual guidance and you gravitate to people who offer you a new view on life, something that makes you stop and think, "Wow, that makes sense," and this can spark a whole new wave of learning and self-improvement where you can become more compassionate.

This is a time for showing leadership in your own life and this means predicting your personality in a positive assertive way. Be more forceful, don't be afraid to go after what you want and get your needs met. This is an excellent time to make an impression on other people and it's also important for you to work on projects where you will feel immediate gratification. There's nothing wrong right now with wanting results immediately, and you should proceed with a lot of confidence and gusto.

October is certainly a time to show purposeful determination, to get your needs met and to elevate yourself above any misguided sense of duty to other people and other things, as your first duty is to yourself.

Marriage and Family

With Jupiter retrograde in Taurus, in your solar eighth house, it's time for you and your partner to break free from some negative emotional patterns or addictions that are creating barriers that stand in the way of you guys developing stronger, deeper bonds and more fulfilling intimacy.

This may be a good time to put some of your relationship issues on the back burner, there is a sense in which you want to avoid the truth about your relationships and are reluctant to deal with reality, but in a sense it may be best to let the dust settle and allow more information to come to light before you make these decisions. So where normally I wouldn't advise being an ostrich with your head in the sand, when it comes to love this month, this can actually work. So delaying tactics and procrastination when it comes to relationship issues could be a good thing, simply because nothing much can be achieved now anyway.

Money

Sheer determination can help improve profits or your ability to promote your products or get positive attention for yourself. However, you do have to be careful of burning bridges, often success now comes at a cost that is not foreseeable until later on. So you have to be careful that being overt and ambitious in your actions now doesn't sting you in the tail later.

Mass communication and the ability to find rare pieces of information or understand and analyze things better than others leads to success and profit.

Living and Loving to the Full

Change is a theme, as are new beginnings, and your mission is to provide others, including your partner, with inspiration and optimism as well. You're magnetic and people are drawn to you because they are capable of seeing the warm and beautiful energy which you bring into their lives. You are also in a position in which you are capable of sharing your qualities as well as achievements with other people. You radiate love and affection towards those you care about the most.

Life is currently particularly good, and the sun is shining your way as you reach the goals that you set.

Planetary Cautions

This is an important time to take personal responsibility, it's important for Libra to become self-aware and break the chains that come with addiction and regressive habits. This is not a time to avoid things or run in circles.

You should not look for easy answers, as habits are hard to break and it takes concerted effort.

You must be prepared to make the long necessary changes which although painful will pay off in the end as you will rediscover your true self.

Self-assessment is important in October, and Libra needs to take some time to list all of the things that you need to purge yourself from, and once that has been achieved, you can embark on the difficult journey of self-improvement.

Moon Magic

The new moon phase extends from the 14th of October to the 28th of October. This waxing phase is the perfect fortnight for new initiatives, setting plans, establishing goals, starting anything prospective and being proactive. This is the action phase, details below:

An excellent period for group goals. Large events and conferences are favored. A good time for social and political goals. New legislation should benefit your aims. Good for new platonic friendships and expanding your social power. Social media activities are successful.

Not the best waxing phase for new careers, job applications or interviews. PR and public speaking are not successful. Becoming self-employed or being entrepreneurial is not advisable.

This is a tricky period for property and home improvements, also a difficult period for entertaining with the family and hosting family events or having family to stay.

Essence and Energies – "And you can dance For inspiration"

During this time, it's very important to use positive affirmations. This is quite a lucky phase and you can capitalize on that by reprogramming your thoughts to focus on positive outcomes. It's vital now to arrest bad habits particularly when they pertain to negative thought patterns and negative feelings about yourself.

The power of attraction works very strongly right now, so devote time to use positive affirmations, especially when it comes to money, increasing your income and having success in terms of getting any loans or grants that you are looking for.

It's important to cultivate a generous spirit and also gratitude in your life, as these can help increase your financial luck. It's also important to release any negative thoughts regarding bitterness or resentment towards others, and you must resist the inclination to be envious as it can be a thorn in your side right now. Focus on your own potential talents and unique experience and don't be envious of others, it's a waste of energy.

Affirmation: "Luck comes my way as I am generous of spirit and I appreciate the abundance in the universe."

Love and Romance

This is an excellent time of the year for you to get involved in new romantic activities, although you are busy you're also meeting a lot more people socially and within work as there are more relaxed, social occasions and the chance to hobnob with colleagues.

This can also be a time when internet dating, dating apps or long distance relationships work really well for you, you enjoy the communication side of these relationships and find it very stimulating and pleasantly distracting to be finding little romantic messages on your texts or message apps.

One problem right now is that although new romance develops, it can be quite superficial, so you're not necessarily getting to know people at a deep level. It's more about sharing laughs, becoming comfortable with each other, gauging each other's sense of humor but nothing particularly deep will be shared this month and there's nothing wrong with that.

Career and Aspiration

Mercury going into Sagittarius indicates quite a lot of mental restlessness, this is a good time for learning new skills, studying information and developing strategies. You are stimulated by activities that involve problem-solving, debating and formulating communications.

This is an excellent time for you to fine-tune your databases, make sure your website is functioning properly and update your email lists. Right now communication and free-flowing communication are essential to you making money, so you want to ensure that you are reaching the maximum audience with your sales pitch or your message, and you also want to make that a two-way street where you can get feedback from clients and customers.

It's very important for you this month to be reactive and not dogmatic, so it's more important to listen to criticism and advice and adjust to changing circumstances, rather than to persist in a pigheaded way doing things in the same old as way innovation and versatility is key.

Adventure and Motivation

This can be a great month for you to learn a new skill and this often helps you combat some of your restless, curious energy and channels it into something that is productive and useful.

So you may want to enroll in a course in a local college to learn about computer programming, a new foreign language or you may want to improve your golf swing by getting professional advice.

You gain a great deal of satisfaction through fine-tuning talents, picking up new skills etc. and while you are learning these romantic opportunities can come about.

This is an excellent month for entertaining and socializing, if you have any invites to go to parties it's definitely time to do so, but it's also great for mixing business with pleasure. So November is a wonderful time to entertain clients or to get closer to colleagues in order to improve your business prospects next year. This is an excellent time to win friends and influence people you are at your most charming, diplomatic and persuasive.

Marriage and Family

In marriage, it's time to renew the levels of affection and physical tenderness, so Libra and your partner should try to get physically close, whether it's watching TV next to each other holding hands or doing other activities like dancing were you are more likely to have physical contact. Often couples become quite cold with each other physically and that can lead to losing touch emotionally.

Touch doesn't have to be sexual, it can just be a tender way of showing concern and support and you should use that, as well as being more aware of your body language in general. You should use mirroring and positive body language, instead of adopting poses which show that you are closed off and perhaps indifferent.

Non-verbal forms of communication are very important in marriage, while in dating and romance you enjoy communicating via text message and electronic forms, in marriage it's important to show your love through your body language, and you can use this to show awareness of your partner's feeling and also to show compassion.

You need to incorporate the level of action, desire and physical satisfaction in the relationship with the underlying issues that are ongoing. So it's important to be sensitive and diplomatic or cognizant of any issues you and your partner are having, while still trying to maintain some romance. So it's not a case of sweeping everything under the carpet in order to have fun or sexual satisfaction, it's more about understanding the totality of the circumstances, but still making sure that the affection and desire is not totally pushed to the side and lost, because it can be an important part of escapism.

Money and Romance

This may be a time where you seek the advice of bankers or people involved in professional money and investment management. Even if you are already in the investment field yourself, you may seek people more experienced than you or who have different areas of expertise so that you can expand your knowledge.

This is a good time for any investments provided they are done very cautiously and conservatively and do not involve a lot of speculation or risk.

You may find that you are able to increase income via becoming a committee or board member, or teaching on the side often yields extra profit if you are looking for a side hustle.

Living and Loving to the Full

Enhancing love magic this month is very much about sensuality, touch and ambience.

Not to sound too corny, but this is definitely is a month where a good old-fashioned candle lit dinner, a bottle of red and bunch of flowers with suitable music tends to work really well, so when it comes to romance, the key is go traditional and you can't go wrong.

Actions speak louder than words this month, so it's all about following through with tangible signs of love. It's a very important month for gifting and those can be expensive gifts, maybe like jewelry, or less expensive gifts like chocolates and flowers but everything counts.

Planetary Cautions

This is a tricky month because with Venus in Libra there's an inclination for you to take your foot off the gas to relax and look for the easy way out, however it's very important right now for you to stay focused and not to let things slip.

Sure you could easily take a weekend off you and enjoy romance and relaxation, but it's not actually a good time to settle down and relax more generally because there is a lot going on and you need to keep abreast of it, as if you step away for too long, you can lose touch and lose sight of the opposition.

It's easy for you to be distracted by novelty and indulgences, you've got your eye out for things that can pique your interest or provide some titillation, so you need to set yourself schedules and keep to your diary or agenda, so there's nothing important which gets missed as your concentration is not always what it should be.

Moon Magic

The new moon phase extends from the 13th of November to the 27th of November. This waxing phase is the perfect fortnight for new initiatives, setting plans, establishing goals, starting anything prospective and being proactive. This is the action phase, details below:

This waxing phase again is not ideal for networking and group goals. Arranging large social events is not advisable. It's not a good time to go with the crowd. Being an individual is important. Social media and scientific goals may not be successful. This is not ideal for social, humanitarian or political goals, also not favorable for attending very large events. The waxing phase is not great for leadership, public speaking and public events. It's not great for new careers or job interviews.

This is an excellent time for spiritual and philosophical pursuits. It's a great time for doing reading and working on your own personal development. It may be a good time for positive thinking, and it's an excellent time for positive vialization and affirmations.

It's also favorable for international travel and your educational goals. Publishing and advertising is successful.

Not a great phase for dating, new romance or parties aimed at meeting people. New entertainment or leisure activities are not favored in the waxing phase.

DECEMBER

Essence and Energies – "I've had my share of sand kicked in my face, but I've come through!"

This is an important phase of realization and acceptance, you then need to make changes or alternatively accept that circumstances have changed and cannot be reversed, but also to realize it's for the better, even if you have to let go of what may have really mattered to you up until now.

The elimination of what is no longer appropriate or necessary is important for your progress to continue. The more you move away from what's no longer working, the more clearly you see what is essential,

Situations especially those involving others (family, friends and work) can come to a head and you should go with it rather than trying to pour oil over troubled water as it your nature response. Help bring the core of any issue to the forefront and do so fearlessly.

Although you may encounter unexpected situations which may increase conflict, this usually encourage you to recognize what really matters to you, this thus increases the authenticity of your life

Affirmation: "I chose to engage with conflict creatively to explore the heart of the matter."

Love and Romance

This is quite a passionate time for both new and existing romances, your desire level is much higher, you're more affectionate, more interested in intimacy and this can be quite an enjoyable time to get to know each other at a deep level, and to begin quite a rewarding sexual experience together.

Libra is quite passionate in 2023 and at the month this passion really explodes in terms of the bedroom in new relationships, so this is an excellent time to take relationships to a new level, and it's not just about sex because there's a spiritual connection happening as well that makes the relationship rather exciting and holistically fulfilling.

If you are single you will have a strong desire for companionship for the warmth and validation of a relationship, and your ability to draw people into your life is enhanced and can make things happen. However there can be some indecision in love as you will likely attract a wide variety of people into your life and it can be hard to sort the wheat from the chaff. What looks good at the moment may not stand the test of time, as you sometimes settle for appearances more than substance.

In stable partnerships, you may experience a greater desire for freedom and change. Travel and other activities together are necessary to keep you satisfied or you could become snappy and irritable. Too much familiarity in relationships can lead to contempt not content and so address any ruts or dull routines.

New relationships that come about now develop very quickly, although you do have to be careful of a certain amount of possessiveness, because it's highly likely due to the intensity of feeling that both you and a new partner will suffer bouts of jealousy, which can make the relationship little bit volatile.

Career and Aspiration

During this month you are likely to be challenged and you have to adapt your thinking quite quickly, you may get criticism or push back on your ideas and you do have to be able to argue your point or justify yourself.

It's very important for you to conduct good record keeping and have your facts at hand, so it's easy for you to be able to explain your point of view or your decision making process to other people.

This can be a very good time for you to test out your ideas and get feedback in order to fine tune to these ideas.

This is a good time for data gathering and doing surveys or market research, because a lot of the results will actually surprise you leading to quite a few adjustments.

The best way to tackle problems this month, with people especially, is not head on. You should play your cards close to your chest and keep your true motivations to yourself until the last minute. What I mean is act strategically, do not be an open book, but be a mystery to those you deal with or with those whom you confront. Am incremental approach is also favored – in any situation play within yourself and do not put it all out there. In a similar way that the Party not in power in government want to keep some policies secret so they do not get hijacked by the ruling party, this is something you should bear in mind. At work make sure that others do not get credit for what you have done or ride off the back of your hard work – this is why some degree of coyness is vital.

Adventure and Motivation

This month you may enjoy spoiling yourself by buying yourself something that you have wanted for a very, very long time. You may choose to buy an antique, a piece of memorabilia, precious metals or stones or some piece of art.

You can have a huge amount of fun shopping around, going to auctions, or going to trade fairs where you can purchase a very specific item that you had had your eye on for a while or maybe for most of your life.

So purchasing products in general, whether they are special sexy items for your wife, or long sought-after things that you're been interested in for a while, or brand new to market gadgets, may bring you a lot of excitement and pleasure.

Marriage and Family

During thus phase, you really have to think before you speak you're not always your diplomatic self simply because you can be a lot more stubborn and often tends to speak before you knows all the facts which can lead to some arguments.

Libra is a little bit stressed out at the moment and often you overthink things, so the key in marriage is to clear up any misconceptions as soon as they arise, otherwise they can leave a bad taste in your mouth, which can lead to you being a little aloof or even hurt when it's not at all necessary.

Libra is not your most compromising, you can be slightly more anal and you tend to be a little bit set in your ways, so there are some issues on which you appears to be making a fuss about nothing, but it may be the case that you're just a little bit more sensitive this time of year and more easily triggered.

Money and Finance

This is quite a prosperous time of year, it should be a good year end for your business and for receiving some bonuses, there may be some unexpected injections of cash which enable you to splash out on special purchases.

You tend to feel quite generous right now and you will be certainly be spoiling those who you love, even if finances do not allow you to be too extravagant, you will still do what you can to make sure the special people in your life receive gifts and are made to feel special.

Libra who sell luxury goods or promote them as part of their business are especially prosperous.

Living and Loving to the Full

You have a lot of passion and power that you can use positively to supercharge your thoughts and affirmations. It's important to think positive, to be proactive and to seize the initiative. When it comes to a situation from work to health, it's vital to have a positive attitude and this can shift the dial.

Many couples or families have Christmas traditions, so Libra and your partner should focus strongly on of these this year. If you don't have any traditions maybe it's time to start developing Christmas traditions or end of year traditions (if you don't celebrate Christmas) can be a very important way of establishing a relationship ritual which makes the relationship more rewarding and uniting, and can also help you both to create treasured memories.

Planetary Cautions

After the 13th of the month Mercury goes retrograde in Capricorn, so it's best to have completed all errands and shorter journeys before then, it's also good to tie up any loose ends regarding contracts or negotiation before that time or they will drag into next year.

After the 13th is not a good time for house hunting or property deals, it's also not a good time to move home or organize renovations to your home.

Inviting guests over to stay after the 13th can also be more hassle than it's worth, and can add a lot to holiday stress.

Moon Magic

The new moon phase extends from the 12th of December to the 26th of December. This waxing phase is the perfect fortnight for new initiatives, setting plans, establishing goals, starting anything prospective and being proactive. This is the action phase, details below:

This waxing phase again is not ideal for social media marketing and group activities. Networking, political activities and joining new organizations is not generally advisable. Leadership and major career changes are not advisable. PR and public events are also not favored.

This is a great time for new websites, IT projects, communication with clients and customers. Careers connected to journalism, travel and teaching are favored. Excellent for short journeys, cyber dating and long distance love.

Great time for competitive activities and making new starts in your personal life. Dealing with animals is favored, this a good month for a radical new diet or fitness regime. Self-improvement and physical therapy or physiotherapy is successful. Recruiting staff or outsourcing is favored. Good for passive income like royalties, donations and gifts.

Well that's a wrap of my biggest most comprehensive Libra Horoscope yet.

Whether you are a Libra or know a Libra, I do believe you will have found this very helpful and informative.

I aim to give you a variety of advice based on psychology, spiritual insight, relationship advice and business guidance, so you get a little bit of everything.

Take care and have a wonderful 2023.

Blessings, Lisa.

Printed in Great Britain
by Amazon

16085641R00058